BRET HARTE

FROM A PAINTING BY JOHN PETTIE, R.A.
PHOTOGRAPH BY FRADELLE & YOUNG, LONDON.

BRET HARTE

BY HENRY W. BOYNTON

 BOOKS FOR LIBRARIES PRESS
FREEPORT, NEW YORK

First Published 1903

Reprinted 1970

INTERNATIONAL STANDARD BOOK NUMBER:

0-8369-5545-5

LIBRARY OF CONGRESS CATALOG CARD NUMBER:

70-133513

PRINTED IN THE UNITED STATES OF AMERICA

CONTENTS

BRET HARTE

I

LIFE

Though Bret Harte was not an old man when he died, the best of his life and work was lived and done a generation ago. He had one brilliant vision and spent the rest of his life in reminding himself of it. In consequence, it ought to be easier than it often can be with one who has died so recently to arrive at something like a fair estimate of his total effectiveness. Not much has been done toward this so far. Bret Harte's death called forth all sorts of newspaper judgments, and a so-called biography, which proved to be at once perfunctory and fulsome. The purpose of the present sketch is to consider soberly what sort of man Bret Harte really was, and what, being that sort of man, he really did.

Francis Brett Harte was born in Albany, N. Y., August 25, 1839. He is said to have had English, German, and Hebrew blood in his veins. His father was "professor" of Greek in the Albany Female College, which was apparently a girls' seminary of the old type. The boy in early years was not robust, and his father was sensible enough to keep him away from school routine for a time. He had learned to read, however, and was not kept away from books; and he was not slower than other boys in getting up an appetite for stories. Beginning at seven with "Dombey and Son," he made his way presently, *via* Dickens, pretty well

[4]

through the itinerary of the English novel. Luckily at that time the "juvenile" had not yet been invented by the senile, nor had Smollett and Fielding been put out of reach on the upper shelves of the family library. [Bret Harte began to write fiction with the best English models before him; though, as we shall see, his work as a whole was based not upon the best of the fiction with which he was familiar, but rather, as was natural for a talent not quite of the first kind, upon the fiction which was most popular in his day.

There was nothing unusual in this boyish fondness for stories, or in any other quality which the boy showed; not even, alas, in his production, at the age of eleven, of some verses which were good enough to be printed in a New York journal. The parents, it appears, disapproved of this effusion, not so much because it was bad verse as because they considered poets rather disreputable persons and feared that the son might turn out to be one.

He had in due time four or five years of common-school instruction; it was all over before his fifteenth year, and he never had any more instruction of any kind. He does not appear, at any time, to have expressed regret for his lack of academic training. We may as well take it for granted that there was nothing for him to regret. What a man might have done under different circumstances is as much a matter of surmise as what he might have done with a different character and endowment. Bret Harte's nature was assimilative rather than acquisitive; his mind followed the line of least resistance, and if one is to guess at all, one may as well guess that university training could have done little for him. In this, as in several other respects, he resembled Irving and Dickens, the two writers whose influence upon him is most apparent, especially in his early work. Like them, he seems to have had the faculty in youth of foregathering with the books and the people that could be of greatest use to him. And it was during precisely the years which he would naturally have spent in the seclusion of college life that

[7]

he was able to assimilate most from the open world.

At all events, the father's death left this boy of fifteen no choice but to find something to do for a living. In 1854 he and his mother undertook the journey to California by way of the Isthmus of Panama. Here one is faced by one of the little mysteries in Bret Harte's life which ordinary inquiry fails to solve. It would have been quite natural that, left an orphan at fifteen, he should, like any other unattached penniless American boy of the period, have turned West in the trail of the forty-niners. All manner of golden fables were making their way eastward, and irresistibly luring the unemployed to try their hand at the new game. But this boy was not an orphan, his mother had to go with him, and the hardships of the journey West made it not a light undertaking for a woman. One speculates a little as to which took the other. Was the boy over-eager for her endurance? or did they, as one rumor goes, follow an older son who had gone to the mines? She does not cumber our narrative long; we hear of her as having lived at Oakland with her son for a time, and after that we hear nothing.

San Francisco, where the boy first looked unsuccessfully for work, was not by this time the most romantic spot in California, in its open and confessed character. So far as its legislative enactments and journalistic pronunciamentos indicated, it might have been a model town according to the Anglo-Saxon convention; a town eager to forget its frontier habits, absorbed in the consideration of its own dignity, and gravely bent upon the attainment of rank as a centre of civilisation. Beneath the surface, and not far beneath, it was as picturesque and lawless as any lover of raw humanity could have desired it to be. Young Frank Harte did not find a fortune ready to his hand there (did not, in fact, find any sort of profitable "job"), but he did see the city pretty thoroughly; and in a surprisingly short time had begun to form the impression of California life which was, after a time, to make his literary fortune.

The conditions of life in San Francisco must have seemed strangely varied to a boy who had been brought up in the staid old Dutch town of Albany. There was the pioneer from the East settling into Western citizenship; the old Spanish resident and, a more important fact, his daughter; the " Heathen Chinee"; the professional gambler; the miner come to town to get rid of his gold-dust: nearly all the types, in short, which later became the writer's stock-in-trade.

But Bret Harte had for some time yet no suspicion of the use which he was to make of his experiences. He was not going about with a note-book looking for "copy." He was looking for a living, and in the meantime enjoying every experience for its own sake. California in the fifties was a place in which experience might be had very readily, if not very cheaply. Not finding any means of supporting himself and his mother in San Francisco, he presently set out on foot for Sonora, Calaveras County, where he set up a school. The experiment, like other early experiments, was not especially successful, except as it gave him the opportunity for new impressions. What some of these impressions were he has himself recorded:

[Here I was thrown among the strangest social conditions that the latter-day world has perhaps seen. The setting was itself heroic. The great mountains of the Sierra Nevada lifted majestic, snow-capped peaks against a sky of purest blue. Magnificent pine forests of trees which were themselves enormous gave to the landscape a sense of largeness and greatness. It was a land of rugged cañons, sharp declivities, and magnificent distances. Amid rushing waters and wildwood freedom, an army of strong men, in red shirts and top-boots, were feverishly in search of the buried gold of earth. Nobody shaved, and hair, moustaches, and beards were untouched by shears or razor. Weaklings and old men were unknown. It took a stout heart and a strong frame to dare the venture, to brave the journey of 3,000 miles and battle for life in the wilds. It was a civilisation composed entirely of young men,

for on one occasion, I remember, an
elderly man—he was fifty, perhaps, but
he had a gray beard—was pointed out as
a curiosity in the city, and men turned in
the street to look at him as they would
have looked at any other unfamiliar ob-
ject.

"These men, generally speaking, were
highly civilised, many of them being cul-
tured and professionally trained. They
were in strange and strong contrast with
their surroundings, for all the trammels
and conventionalities of settled civilisation had been left thousands of miles be-
hind. It was a land of perfect freedom,
limited only by the instinct and the habit
of law which prevailed in the mass. All
its forms were original, rude, and pictu-

resque. /Woman was almost unknown, and enjoyed the high estimation of a rarity./ The chivalry natural to manhood invested her with ideal value when respect could supplement it, and with exceptional value even when it could not. Strong passions brought quick climaxes, all the better and worse forces of manhood being in unbridled play. ⌈To me it was like a strange, ever-varying panorama, so novel that it was difficult to grasp comprehensively. In fact, it was not till years afterward that the great mass of primary impressions on my mind became sufficiently clarified for literary use."/

The lad had one qualification for school-teaching, though he can hardly have had any other—an understanding of children. Oddly enough, his literary treatment of childish character is less sentimental than his handling of adult character. Probably the routine of school-life was bitter enough to the taste of one who was himself little better than "a truant schoolboy," to use his own phrase. The hard manual labor and the modest returns of placer mining, as he tried it a little later, were not more to his taste; and before, at the age of nineteen, he returned to San Francisco he had hard experience as a tax-collector, a Wells-Fargo Express messenger, a druggist's assistant, and a compositor. Many of his subsequent tales turned upon these early experiences, though more of them have to do with what he saw and heard than with what he did. And what he did was of even less profit to his pocket. When presently he returned to San Francisco, he was still in search of employment, and only his experience as compositor proved of value to him; it got him the chance to set type in the composing-room of *The Golden Era.*

"The Golden Era," says Mr. Charles Warren Stoddard, "was the cradle and grave of many a high hope—there was nothing to be compared with it that side of the Mississippi; and though it could point with pride—it never failed to do so —to a somewhat notable line of contributors, it had always the fine air of the amateur. . . . I remember his [the editor's] calling my attention to a certain

anonymous contribution, just received, and nodding his head prophetically, for he already had his eye on its fledgling author, a young compositor on the floor above. It was Bret Harte's first appearance in *The Golden Era*."

Of the quality of the audience to which *The Golden Era* addressed itself, Bret Harte gave, late in life, a surprisingly flattering account. His earlier efforts, he says, "were addressed to an audience half foreign in their sympathies, and still imbued with Eastern or New England habits and literary traditions. 'Home' was still potent with these voluntary exiles in their moments of relaxation. Eastern magazines and current Eastern literature formed their literary recreation,

[18]

and the sale of the better class of periodicals was singularly great. Nor was this taste confined to American literature. The illustrated and satirical English journals were as frequently seen in California as in Massachusetts; and the author records that he has experienced more difficulty in procuring a copy of *Punch* in an English provincial town than was his fortune at 'Red Dog' or 'One-Horse Gulch.' An audience thus liberally equipped and familiar with the best modern writers was naturally critical and exacting, and no one appreciates more than he does the salutary effects of this severe discipline upon his earlier efforts."

It may be wrong to imagine that memory tinged the facts with a rosy bloom.

The means by which this critical and exacting temper expressed itself were, at least, not always Eastern or academic. The first book with which Bret Harte had to do was an anthology of Californian verse. Here is one of the salutary and severe notices which, according to the author's own account, it received — a "tempered" version, moreover:

"The hogwash and purp-stuff ladled out from the slop-bucket of Messrs. ——— and Co., of Frisco, by some lop-eared Eastern apprentice, and called 'A Compilation of Californian Verse,' might be passed over, so far as criticism goes. A club in the hands of any able-bodied citizen of Red Dog and a steamboat ticket to the Bay, cheerfully contributed from this office, would be all-sufficient. But when an imported greenhorn dares to call his flapdoodle mixture 'Californian,' it is an insult to the State that has produced the gifted 'Yellow Hammer,' whose lofty flights have, from time to time, dazzled our readers in the columns of *The Jay Hawk*. That this complacent editorial jackass, browsing among the docks and thistles which he has served up in this volume, should make no allusion to California's greatest bard is rather a confession of his idiocy than a slur upon the genius of our esteemed contributor."

Whatever may be true of the general literacy and refinement of that early California, there is no doubt that San Francisco contained men of literary ability.

At the moment of Harte's connection with *The Golden Era* the city possessed a group of vigorous young journalists, most of whom had literary ambition. Among them were Mark Twain, Charles Warren Stoddard, Prentice Mulford, and Charles Henry Webb. Largely to provide a vehicle for their theories and their work, *The Californian* was founded. The journal did not live long, in spite of the unusual quality of its staff. Its epitaph has been neatly phrased by Mr. Howells. "These ingenuous young men," he says, "with the fatuity of gifted people, had established a literary newspaper in San Francisco, and they brilliantly co-operated to its early extinction."

Among the casual presences attracted

by that old California was a certain Sam Clemens, who had begun to write over the signature of Mark Twain, but had received no general recognition. Curiously enough, it was through Bret Harte and *The Californian* that his first hit was made. A month after their first meeting Mr. Clemens called on Harte, who tells this story: "He had been away in the mining districts on some newspaper assignment in the meantime. In the course of conversation he remarked that the unearthly laziness that prevailed in the town he had been visiting was beyond anything in his previous experience. He said the men did nothing all day long but sit around the bar-room stove, spit, and 'swop lies.' He spoke in a slow, rather

satirical drawl, which was in itself irre-
sistible. He went on to tell one of those
extravagant stories, and half uncon-
sciously dropped into the lazy tone and
manner of the original narrator. I asked
him to tell it again to a friend who came
in, and then asked him to write it out for
The Californian. He did so, and when
published it was an emphatic success. It
was the first work of his that had attracted general attention, and it crossed
the Sierras for an Eastern reading. The
story was 'The Jumping Frog of Calaveras.' It is now known and laughed
over, I suppose, wherever the English
tongue is spoken; but it will never be as
funny to anyone in print as it was to me,
told for the first time by the unknown

Twain himself on that morning in the San Francisco Mint."

Bret Harte was at this time secretary to the superintendent of the United States Mint, and also had a place upon the staff of *The Golden Era,* to which, upon the collapse of *The Californian,* Mark Twain became a frequent contributor. Most of Harte's own work during this period was purely journalistic in effect, though he had already produced prose and verse of a literary quality.

His most decisive step from journalism to literature was made when, in 1868, he became the editor of the newly founded *Overland Monthly.* In the second number appeared "The Luck of Roaring Camp," the first and the most famous of

[25]

his short stories. It is worth while to quote somewhat fully from the author's own account of the circumstances under which the story was printed, and of the reception which it met:

"When the first number of the *Overland Monthly* appeared the author, then its editor, called the publisher's attention to the lack of any distinctively Californian romance in its pages, and averred that, should no other contribution come in, he himself would supply the omission in the next number. No other contribution was offered, and the author, having the plot and the general idea in his mind, in a few days sent the manuscript of 'The Luck of Roaring Camp' to the printer. He had not yet received the proof-sheets when he was suddenly summoned to the office of the publisher, whom he found standing, the picture of dismay and anxiety, with the proof before him. The indignation and stupefaction of the author can be well understood when he was told that the printer, instead of returning the proofs to him, had submitted them to the publisher, with the emphatic declaration that the matter there was so indecent, irreligious, and improper that his proofreader—a young lady—had with difficulty been induced to continue its perusal, and that he, as a friend of the publisher, and a well-wisher of the magazine, was impelled to present to him personally this shameless evidence of the manner in which the editor was imperilling the future usefulness of that enterprise." The publisher and others who read the story were inclined to agree that it ought not to appear in the *Overland Monthly.* "Finally the story was submitted to three gentlemen of culture and experience, friends of publisher and author, who were unable, however, to come to any clear decision. It was, however, suggested to the author that, assuming the natural hypothesis that his editorial reasoning might be warped by his literary predilections in a consideration of one of his own productions, a personal sacrifice would at this juncture be in the last degree heroic. This last suggestion had the effect of ending all further discussion, for he at once informed the publisher that the question of the propriety of the story was no longer at issue; the only question was of his capacity to exercise the proper editorial judgment, and that unless he was permitted to test that capacity by the publication of the story, and abide squarely by the result, he must resign his editorial position."

Of course the story was printed, and, except among the unco guid and a class of Californians who thought the dignity of California ought to be upheld if necessary at the expense of truth, scored a great success. In the Eastern States and in England the response was immediate and enthusiastic. One of the most flattering signs of its success was a letter from Fields, Osgood & Co., publishers of

The Atlantic Monthly, asking for a story in the vein of "The Luck of Roaring Camp."

At first this general approbation had a good effect. "Thus encouraged," he wrote many years later, " 'The Luck of Roaring Camp' was followed by 'The Outcasts of Poker Flat,' 'Miggles,' 'Tennessee's Partner,' and those various other characters who had impressed the author when, a mere truant schoolboy, he had lived among them. It is hardly necessary to say to any observer of human nature that at this time he was advised by kind and well-meaning friends to content himself with the success of the 'Luck,' and not tempt criticism again; or from that moment ever after he was in receipt of

[30]

that equally sincere contemporaneous criticism which assured him gravely that each successive story was a falling off from the last. Howbeit, by reinvigorated confidence in himself and some conscientious industry, he managed to get together in a year six or eight of these sketches, which, in a volume called 'The Luck of Roaring Camp and other Sketches,' gave him that encouragement in America and England that has since seemed to justify him in swelling these records of a picturesque passing civilisation into the compass of the present edition.

"A few words regarding the peculiar conditions of life and society that are here rudely sketched, and often but barely outlined. The author is aware that, partly from a habit of thought and expression, partly from the exigencies of brevity in his narratives, and partly from the habit of addressing an audience familiar with the local scenery, he often assumes, as premises already granted by the reader, the existence of a peculiar and romantic state of civilisation, the like of which few English readers are inclined to accept without corroborative facts and figures. These he could only give by referring to the ephemeral records of Californian journals of that date and the testimony of far-scattered witnesses, survivors of the exodus of 1849. He must beg the reader to bear in mind that this emigration was either across a continent almost

unexplored or by the way of a long and
dangerous voyage around Cape Horn,
and that the promised land itself pre-
sented the singular spectacle of a patri-
archal Latin race who had been left to
themselves, forgotten by the world, for
nearly three hundred years. The faith,
courage, vigour, youth, and capacity for
adventure necessary to this emigration
produced a body of men as strongly distinctive as the companions of Jason. Un-
like most pioneers, the majority were men
of profession and education; all were
young, and all had staked their future in
the enterprise. Critics who have taken
large and exhaustive views of mankind
and society from club windows in Pall
Mall or the Fifth Avenue can only accept

for granted the turbulent chivalry that
thronged the streets of San Francisco in
the gala day of her youth, and must read
the blazon of their deeds like the doubtful
quarterings of the shield of Amadis de
Gaul. The author has been frequently
asked if such and such incidents were real
—if he had ever met such and such characters. To this he must return the same
answer, that in only a single instance was
he conscious of drawing purely from his
imagination and fancy for a character
and a logical succession of incidents
drawn therefrom. A few weeks after his
story was published he received a letter,
authentically signed, *correcting some of
the minor details of his facts* (?) and en-
closing as corroborative evidence a slip

from an old newspaper, wherein the main
incident of his supposed fanciful creation
was recorded with a largeness of statement that far transcended his powers of
imagination."

His first great success was quickly followed by his second; it could not have
occurred to anybody then that there could
never be any further successes of the same
rank. "Plain Language from Truthful
James," or, as it came to be called, "The
Heathen Chinee," at once gained a no-
toriety even wider than his short stories
had won. Like "The Luck of Roaring
Camp," it aroused only mild interest in
San Francisco, but in the East and in
England it was hailed with delight.
After the passage of a generation it re-

mains one of the best known humorous poems in the language; its phraseology has even attained the secondary fame of being familiar to thousands who do not know the whole poem. The author himself grew a little tired of the excessive popularity of a mere *jeu d'esprit*.

Some light is thrown upon his character, as well as upon the history of these famous verses, in the following item from the *San Francisco News-Letter*, written shortly after Harte's death:

"Slow of speech and thought, he never could be depended upon to supply copy on time to his printer. For a period he was supposed to be a regular contributor to the columns of this paper, but he was never a 'regular' contributor to any paper. On one occasion, after a silence of two or three weeks, he suddenly recalled his duty to the *News-Letter,* and going through some manuscript, selected a short poem and handed it in to this office. The late Mr. Marriott, who was conceded to be an excellent judge of poetry, rejected it, asserting that it was 'twaddle.' About a year afterward Mr. Harte, being hard up for copy, as he usually was, published his rejected poem in the *Overland Monthly,* of which he had become editor. It made the writer famous in a day, for it was none other than 'The Heathen Chinee,' which was soon in everybody's mouth. This writer afterward asked Mr. Marriott how he came to reject so popular a success. He replied that 'it was evident that the best might sometimes be mistaken.' The fact was that by his dilatoriness Mr. Harte had become *persona non grata,* and the venerable editor took this way of getting even with him."

We shall have something to say presently of the merit of "The Heathen Chinee." Here we have to consider only its sudden popularity and the effect of that popularity upon its author's career. There is little doubt that it served to clinch the general conviction that Bret Harte was too important a person to live in California.

In the spring of 1870, at all events, the now famous writer left California not to return. He had lived there for sixteen years. Between the ages of fifteen and nineteen, in the course of his miscellaneous experience of California life, he had gathered pretty much all the material for his work. During the next five or six years he was profitably employed in growing old enough to begin to make effective use of this material. Most of his best work was done within two years of his assumption of the *Overland Monthly* editorship. His motives in leaving California at the end of these two years have been a good deal discussed. The plain truth seems to be that his head was turned, and he naturally edged toward the point of the compass from which the applause came loudest. It is impossible not to see weakness in the facility with which he succumbed to the pressure which was brought to bear upon him by Eastern publishers and Eastern admirers.

It is possible, however, that too much has been made of the effect upon his work of his physical removal to the East, and, subsequently, to England. His interpretation of early California life appears to have been complete; very likely if he had remained he would have been unable to make effective literary use of the more complicated conditions which were already developing. Just that one picturesque episode in American life he seems to have been born to understand and to chronicle, and he can hardly be held responsible for having outlived the moment without being able to forget it. Certainly there never came another moment which he knew how to interpret in the same way; and he had, if he was to write at all, to remain for the rest of his life his own copyist, when he did not choose to be the copyist of others.

Before we follow him across the continent to New York it may be worth while to note what sort of place he had made for himself in California. He had gained and held for years a fairly profitable sinecure in the San Francisco Mint; he had gained and held with credit the editorship of the *Overland Monthly;* and he had been invited, not long before his departure for the East, to a chair of literature at the University of California. Such marks of public approbation he had received, and he had made warm personal friends. He had also gained a reputation for that unreliability, so far as meeting engagements and paying debts are concerned, which is supposed (except by employers and creditors) to be an engaging if not virtuous corollary of "the artistic temperament."

With such a nature and with such a fame the young author was not likely to bear himself very wisely during the dangerous process, upon which the public is inclined in such cases to insist, of translation from a personality into a personage. According to the usual fatuous method of publics, his Eastern admirers lost no time in fêting and flattering their idol of the moment beyond the point of reason,

He was introduced to authors' clubs, forced to give a Phi Beta Kappa poem at Harvard (which, naturally, turned out to be rather inadequate), and urged to write for the best magazines. *The Atlantic Monthly* subsidised him, for a time, at a salary of ten thousand dollars a year.

The result was what might have been expected by those who really knew the man. During, we will say, the three years which assisted in the production of the author's strongest and most sincere work he seems to have been inspired by a genuine creative impulse, made more fruitful in its later manifestations by the grateful sense that the world was ready to appreciate the best of what he could give it. This was the period of perfect balance between the working of the creative instinct and the sense of its acceptable worth which, to any but the highest order of creative genius, must be brief. Later, and with a somewhat indecorous suddenness, as it seems to the student of such phenomena, the balance was destroyed. A little flattery, a little money in sight, and the artist (quite innocently, like a child whose head is turned by too much attention) becomes an artisan.

The unreliability which we have noted as characteristic of his career in California became more and more marked during the years immediately following his translation to the East. In San Francisco his life had never wholly lacked the safeguard of routine which is so essential to the productiveness of temperaments like his. He was now his own master, free to do his work as he chose, and unhampered by the pressure of small duties. Consequently he did very little. The salary of ten thousand dollars paid by *The Atlantic Monthly,* for an indefinite number of contributions, proved a very bad speculation, for the *Atlantic.*

In New York he found himself continually more involved in social engagements, and his summers were passed at expensive resorts, such as Cohasset, Lenox, and Newport. He was, in short, growing idle and extravagant, making something of a figure in the world about town, and hardly holding his own in the world of letters. In the course of a few

years he was hopelessly in debt. He
made a good deal of money, by lecturing
as well as by writing, but it was his instinct to live beyond his means. He had
already tasted the joys of the political
sinecure, and when at length a chance
came to lie by for a time in that kind of
safe harbour he was not slow in accepting it. In 1878 he left his family and
his more pressing embarrassments in
America to accept a small Prussian Con-
sulate. "It is to be hoped," wrote the
London *Athenæum,* with unconscious
irony, "that his consular duties at Crefeld will not prove so engrossing as to
prevent him from continuing to write."
Bret Harte was quite incapable of being
inconvenienced by consular duties, either

at Crefeld, or at Glasgow, whither, by the labours of American friends, he presently found himself transferred. It seems, indeed, to be clear that his absorption in the duties of his post at Glasgow was so notoriously a fault of omission that his removal in 1885 was a matter of necessity. The rest of his life he spent in England, and during those seventeen years, though he wrote much, he produced nothing which added materially to his reputation. He died at the country-house of a friend in Surrey, May 5, 1902.

II

PERSONALITY

What, then, is the sum of our impression of Bret Harte's personality? It is safe to say, to begin with, that its chief ingredient was temperament rather than character. There was nothing heroic about the man, either for good or ill. Those boyish experiences of his in California do indicate that he was not deficient in physical courage. He showed constancy, too, in his early attempts at literature, and, in the moment of his first realisation of power, a kind of exaltation which for a time kept him up to the mark. Thereafter, as we have said, he followed the line of least resistance, drifting upon a pleasant tide of approbation, filling, in

the approved way, the literary orders
which unfailingly came to him, and, in
short, making the easiest possible business
of his art and of his life.

Such letters of his as have been published present him, on the whole, in a more
favourable light than one would expect.
They are not only neat and humorous,
they often attract one strongly to the
writer for his own sake. They remind
one that it is not enough to consider a
man's relation to his employers or his
creditors, or even to his work. We have
also to ask what kind of man he was in
the eyes of his friends, and how much he
counted for in their lives.

His domestic experience was not ideal.
He was married just before he reached

the not over-marriageable age of twenty-three, and when he left California there were two children, who were followed later by two more. No open scandal was ever connected with his name, but it is not a secret that for some time before his departure from America his home life was not of the pleasantest. Letters written during a lecturing tour in the West in 1873 show that the break, if break there was, came later. One notices that he talks, as a man may to his wife, a good deal of his inconveniences and his symptoms:

"I did not want to write this disappointment to you as long as there was some prospect of better things. You can imagine, however, how I feel at this cruel loss of time and money—to say nothing of my health, which is still so poor. I had almost recovered from my cold, but while lecturing at Ottawa at the Skating Rink, a hideous, dismal, damp barn—the only available place in town—I caught a fresh cold, and have been coughing badly ever since. And you can well imagine that my business annoyances do not add greatly to my sleep or appetite.

"I make no comment; you can imagine the half-sick, utterly disgusted man who glared at that audience over his desk that night, and d—d them inwardly in his heart."

These letters also contain passages which show that the eye which had been so keen in California days had not grown

dull. Of the society of a Kansas city he
says:

"And, of course, as in all such places,
the women contrast poorly with the men
—even in feminine qualities. Somehow a
man here may wear fustian and glaring
colours and paper collars and yet keep his
gentleness and delicacy, but a woman in
glaring 'Dolly Vardens' and artificial
flowers changes nature with him at once.
I've seen but one that interested me—an
old negro wench. She was talking and
laughing outside my door the other even-
ing, but her laugh was so sweet and unc-
tuous and musical—so full of breadth and
goodness, that I went outside and talked
to her while she was scrubbing the stones.
She laughed as a canary-bird sings—be-

cause she couldn't help it. It did me a world of good, for it was before the lecture, at twilight, when I am very blue and low-tuned. She had been a slave."

His first letters from Crefeld are more than perfunctorily affectionate. He finds himself very lonely and forlorn:

"It's been up-hill work ever since I left New York, but I shall try to see it through, please God! I don't allow myself to think over it at all, or I should go crazy. I shut my eyes to it, and in doing so perhaps I shut out what is often so pleasant to a traveller's first impressions, but thus far London has only seemed to me a sluggish nightmare through which I have waked, and Paris a confused sort of hysterical experience. I had hoped for a little kindness and rest here. Perhaps it may come. To-day I found here (forwarded from London) a kind little response to my card, from Froude, who invites me to come to his country place— an old seaport village in Devonshire. If everything has gone well here—if I can make it go well here—I shall go back to London and Paris for a vacation of a few weeks, and see Froude at last.

"At least, Nan, be sure I've written now the worst; I think things must be better soon. I shall, please God, make some friends in good time, and will try and be patient. But I shall not think of sending for you until I see clearly that I can stay myself. If the worst comes to the worst I shall try to stand it for a year, and save enough to come home and begin anew there. But I could not stand it to see you break your heart here through disappointment, as I mayhap may do."

It would be unfair to suggest that there is deliberate disingenuousness in the closing sentences, yet, allowing for the impersonal loneliness and nostalgia which so naturally belongs to a first experience in a strange land, it is hard to take them quite seriously. Indeed, there is a touch of shrillness about the whole passage which does not quite explain itself. Bret Harte had, like all self-indulgent and sentimental persons, great capacity for self-pity. At all events, after triumphantly "standing" his expatriation for a year, he found it possible to stand it pretty cheerfully for the rest of his life; and the moment at which he could think of sending for his family was postponed with equal success.

The vacation for which he had so pleasantly begun to plan at the first moment of his consular labours was soon effected. A month later he is writing from Froude's estate in Devonshire, and the letter contains a fine burst of enthusiasm about his host:

"But Froude—dear old noble fellow— is splendid. I love him more than I ever did in America. He is great, broad, manly—democratic in the best sense of the word, scorning all sycophancy and meanness, accepting all that is around him, yet more proud of his literary profession than of his kinship with these people whom he quietly controls. There are only a few literary men like him here, but they are Kings. I could not have had a better introduction to them than through Froude, who knows them all, who is Tennyson's best friend, and who is anxious to make my *entrée* among them a success."

A letter written shortly after from London concludes: "I dare not go with Osgood to Liverpool for fear I shall get on the steamer with him and return;" whereupon his adoring biographer remarks: "There is something very pathetic in the picture of the man whose thoughts turned to the West, but whose duties pointed to the East." His duties at the moment pointed somewhat farther east-

ward than London, and after some three
months more of vacation he did make his
way back to Crefeld.

There we presently behold him, become
somewhat domesticated for a time, taking
observations of German life, making a
German friend or two, and listening to
German music. Altogether the most
spirited passage in his letters of this
period describes his first impression of
Wagner, of the probable inadequacy of
which, to be just, he seemed quite aware:

"My first operatic experience was
'Tannhäuser.' I can see your superior
smile, Anna, at this; and I know how you
will take my criticism of Wagner, so I
don't mind saying plainly that it was the
most diabolically hideous and stupidly

monotonous performance I ever heard. I shall say nothing about the orchestral harmonies, for there wasn't anything going on of that kind, unless you call something that seemed like a boiler factory at work in the next street, and the wind whistling through the rigging of a channel steamer, harmony. But *I must say one thing!* In the third act, I think, Tannhäuser and two other minstrels sing before the King and Court to the accompaniment of their harps—and the boiler factory. Each minstrel sang, or rather declaimed, something like the multiplication table for about twenty minutes. Tannhäuser, when his turn came, declaimed longer and more lugubriously and ponderously and monotonously than

the others, and went into 'nine times nine
are eighty-one' and 'ten times two are
twenty,' when suddenly, when they had
finished, they all drew their swords and
rushed at him. I turned to Gen. Von
Rauch and said to him that 'I didn't wonder at it.' 'Ah,' said he, 'you know the
story, then?' 'No, not exactly,' I replied.
'Ja wohl,' said Von Rauch, 'the story is
that these minstrels are all singing in
praise of Love, but they are furious at
Tannhäuser, who loves Hilda the German Venus, for singing in the praise of
Love so *wildly,* so *warmly,* so *passionate-
ly.*' Then I concluded that I really did
not understand Wagner."

Bret Harte, we find, was as prone to
repeat his good things as other good let-

ter-writers. In an early letter from Crefeld he says: "I know now from my observations, both here and in Paris and London, where the scene-painters at the theatres get their subjects. Those impossible houses, those unreal, silent streets, all exist in Europe." Seventeen years later, during his last visit to the Continent, he is struck with the similar spectacularity of the Swiss landscape, and writes (the italics are his own):

"*This* part of Switzerland is entirely new to me. I can only tell you that the two photographs I send you are absolutely *true* in detail and effect, and that the characteristic, and even the defect, of the scenery here is that it looks as if it were *artistically composed;* all the drop-

[61]

curtains, all the stage scenes, all the ballet backgrounds you have ever seen in the theatre exist here *in reality*. The painter has nothing to compose—the photographer still less; that châlet, that terrace, that snow-peak, is exactly *where it ought to be*. The view from my balcony at this moment is a *picture* hanging on my wall —not a view at all. You begin to have a horrible suspicion that Daudet's joke about all 'Switzerland being a gigantic hotel company' is *true*. You hesitate about sitting down on this stone terrace lest it shouldn't be 'practical'; and you don't dare knock at the door of this bright Venetian-awned shop lest it should be only painted canvas. There is a whole street in Montreux that I have seen a dozen

times in Grand Opera. The *people*—
tourists of all nations — are the only
things *real,* and in the hotels, when they
are in full-dress on the balconies or sa-
loons, they look like—*the audience!*"

During his first stay in London, Harte
had arranged for a lecture tour in England which had been a pecuniary failure.
A second experiment, made a little later,
was successful. Apparently he had only
one lecture, which he called "The Argonauts of '49," and which he had delivered
many times in America. The warmth
with which he was received by English
audiences, as well as by English society,
probably made each return to Crefeld
more difficult. Some seven months after
his appointment he writes:

"I am very seriously thinking of asking the department to change my location. Germany is no place for me. I feel it more and more every day. So that if I do not hold out any hopes to you it is because I do not know if I shall stay here. There are so many places better for my health, for my literary plans, for my comfort, and for my purse than this. I shall write quietly to one or two of my Washington friends to see if it can be managed. I shall have made a good head here; by good luck, I fear, more than by management. The consular business will exceed this year any previous year, and I can hand over to the Government quite a handsome sum."

Certainly Germany was not the place

for him. He was unacquainted with the language and literature, and unable to grasp the German point of view and way of life. Yet his work was extremely popular in Germany, appearing to be, in its quality of sentiment, singularly intelligible to the Teutonic mind. "But the Crefeld invoices were not to hold him long in thrall," says the biographer, sympathetically. The Washington friends managed a transfer to Scotland, and for some years Harte was free to be the titular thrall of the Glasgow invoices, and, in practice, to enjoy the ready English hospitality to which he was now welcome. He made many friends among distinguished Englishmen, and in fact found a place in the society of London such as seems never to have been quite open to him in Boston or New York; a not uncommon experience for brilliant Americans abroad. He became intimate also with two literary men, with whom he had much in common, William Black and Walter Besant; was entertained by the Lowells, and corresponded with by John Hay; and there was never a break in his intimacy with Froude.

He formed an even closer intimacy with Monsieur and Madame Van de Velde —the former of the Belgian diplomatic corps, the latter apparently a clever woman of the world. In her house and in the presence of herself "and her attendants," according to the English chronicler, Bret Harte died. His wife and children were present at the funeral, some days later. A newspaper letter of Madame Van de Velde's is worth quoting, as it explains the English attitude toward this American author, and as it throws light upon his own character as others saw it:

"It is difficult for an observant stranger to pass even a short time in Great Britain without becoming aware of a distinctively characteristic trait in the inhabitants, and it is impossible for anyone who has lived a number of years there not to be absolutely convinced of its dominance. The Englishman, in his cold, undemonstrative fashion, is intensely patriotic; in his heart of hearts he firmly believes that in the scheme of creation he was formed out of special clay, while the

[67]

remainder of human beings have been
moulded from a much inferior material.
He is equally sure that no effort of grace
can ever raise the alien to his level; but,
while he is piously grateful for this dis-
pensation of Providence, he recognises
and appreciates the right of an outsider
to maintain an exalted opinion of his own
country and nationality; he respects him
for it even when he endeavours to prove
it erroneous; nay, more, should his argu-
ments successfully establish a recognition
of his own superiority, he immediately
ceases to entertain regard and toleration
for the too easily persuaded stranger.
This thoroughly English and so far hon-
ourable peculiarity is one of the reasons,
apart from his merits as a literary celeb-

rity, why Bret Harte is extremely popular in England, and has always been so.

"Before he took up his residence in London his genius and originality had won him admirers, but when he gave them the opportunity of becoming acquainted with the man, independently, as it were, of the author, they promptly ascertained that no more uncompromising American had ever set foot among them. Time has not dulled Bret Harte's instinctive affection for the land of his birth, for its institutions, its climate, its natural beauties, and, above all, its character and moral attributes of its inhabitants. Even his association with the aristocratic representatives of London society has been impotent to modify his views or to win him over to less independent professions. He is as single-minded to-day as he was when he first landed on British soil. A general favourite in the most diverse circles, social, literary, scientific, artistic, or military, his strong primitive nature and his positive individuality have remained intact. Always polite and gentle, neither seeking nor evading controversy, he is steadfastly unchangeable in his political and patriotic beliefs. He has frequently been heard to express himself frankly on the vexed question of Anglo-American marriages, severely satirising those of his fair compatriots who, dazzled by the lustre of lordly alliances, have too closely assimilated with the land of their adoption, and apparently forgotten their country. To such he has not hesitated to apply the term of 'apostates.' . . .

"It has been several times remarked that the appearance of Bret Harte does not coincide with the preconceived expectations of his readers. They had formed a vague, intangible idea of a wild, reckless Californian, impatient of social trammels, whose life among the Argonauts must have fashioned him after a type differing widely from the reality. These idealists were partly disappointed, partly relieved, when their American visitor turned out to be a quiet, low-voiced, easy-mannered, polished gentleman, who, smiling, confessed that precisely because he had roughed it a good deal in his youth he was inclined to enjoy

the comforts and avail himself of the
facilities of an older civilisation when
placed within his reach. He also gently
intimated that days on the top of a stage-
coach, or on the back of a mustang, and
nights spent at poker, would not materially assist in the writing of stories which
are never produced fast enough to merit
the demand.

"The American humourist has been
represented as sinking into the slough
of sybaritic idleness; as working five
hours before breakfast and recruiting by
violent pedestrian exercise; he changed
his clothes six times a day; he neglected
his personal appearance; he has taken a
big mansion in Norfolk and entertained
on a large scale; he had hidden himself

[72]

in a small cottage in the suburbs; he filled waste-paper baskets with torn notes of invitations; he wrote sheets and sheets of copy; society women booked him months ahead to secure his presence at their receptions; he made thousands of pounds a year; he had ceased to write at all; he had become 'quite English, you know,' and had formally adjured America.

"Singularly enough, many of Bret Harte's countrymen in London did not take the trouble to verify these statements; they accepted them blindly, and thus they may have been reproduced in some American newspapers, together with the account of the last *début* of a brilliant New York belle in London, or the detailed description of some million-aire's festival. . . .

"It has been said that Bret Harte's stories fetch bigger prices in the market than any similar form of literature of the present day. This is perhaps correct, but he does not consider himself justified on that account in relaxing his labours. He has obligations in America, and this claim upon him forms at once the motive and the reason of his prolonged stay in England, in spite of the inclination and desire so strong in his heart to revisit his native land.

"Bret Harte has more than once been asked to lecture in England on English customs and English society, but he has always demurred. He is too grateful for

the welcome tendered to him to risk re-
paying it with apparent discourtesy of
censure; he is too honest and frank to
give indiscriminate praise or to lay himself open to the reproach of flattery.
Some day he may be persuaded to give
the world the result of close, keen, and
impartial observations, and we dare say
he will do so in the spirit of conscientious-
ness and sincerity so characteristic of all
his writings."

Of Bret Harte's modesty it is necessary to say this: that while it is undoubt-
edly true that he shrank from public
attentions requiring his presence and ex-
ertion—while he hated to be talked at by
strangers, and to talk to strangers of
himself—he took his own product, to the

[75]

very end, with quite sufficient seriousness. He did not like to lecture, he did not like to make after-dinner speeches, but he did thoroughly enjoy adulation of a proper and private sort. There is no evidence that he realised the artistic futility of trading upon his early success in the interpretation of Californian life, or that he recognised the failure of his occasional attempts to interpret other phases of life. Why should he? Periodicals and publishers, for thirty years, besieged him with orders for stories, to which, in his own time and to his own profit, he paid the proper tribute of obedience.

As for his patriotism, it need only be said that it was of the amiably truculent sort which is expected of the American abroad. That he ever seriously desired to return to America is a point of mere surmise. He was having a very comfortable existence in England. He could command in America neither the social nor the literary standing which England was glad to give him. From his wife and family (when Madame Van de Velde wrote) he had been for some time estranged. The line of least resistance did not run westward from Liverpool.

There is, in fine, no doubt that Bret Harte was, to casual friends and acquaintances, an amiable and companionable person. Nobody has ever alleged that he had vices, unless weakness is a vice; and an amiable weakness, a willing-

ness to give his friends and his public
what they desired, characterised his life
and his artistic career. The life of English clubs and country-houses evidently
demanded nothing which he was not able
to give, and his public was, unfortunate-
ly, not exacting. So far as it was English, it had a pretty vague notion of the
veracity of his replicas of the early Californian sketches. Nor was judgment in
the Eastern States of America greatly
more discriminating. The man had not
only no trouble in disposing of his wares;
he had more "orders" than he could fill.
So he went down in comfort to the grave,
and his most charitable epitaph would in-
clude, in some form, the statement that,
though his only inspiration was outlived

[78]

by more than thirty years, that was not, directly, his fault; and the remark might fairly be appended that a single inspiration, a single moment of supreme sincerity, is more than is allotted to one in a million of our admirable and progressive species.

III

WORK

It was apparently a good-fortune which led Bret Harte to the field of his one notable success, and an ill-fortune which led him away from it; but there is a tide in the affairs of men, and certainly in this case the important fact is not that the moment of flood came so early and was so brief, but that the man was, after all, able to seize and make the most of it.

With the appearance of "The Luck of Roaring Camp" began the single period in his life which one studies with almost unqualified satisfaction, the period during which, both as man and as artist, his integrity maintained itself quite above fear and above reproach.

The immediate sensation created by "The Luck" has, as some one has said, no parallel in the history of English fiction, except in the instances of "Waverley" and "Pickwick." No other short story ever leaped so suddenly into what proved to be permanent fame. Of course the novelty of its theme had much to do with its first success. The pursuit of local colour and the local type was a comparatively new chase, and hardly before or since have colour and type offered themselves so glowing and salient as in the California which Bret Harte knew. But fidelity to the local fact is a subordinate virtue in the practice of fiction, and it may well be that the public which was startled and delighted by Harte's early

[81]

tales fancied a charm in the accessories of his art which really inhered in its substance. They were fascinated not more by the oddity of the theme than by the author's unmoral attitude toward it; and if in his later work there came to be something a little conscious, even spectacular, in his maintenance of that attitude, the fact was evidently due to the belabouring he had received at the hands of well-meaning moral persons. Eventually he thought it worth while to formulate a defence of what had been in the beginning an instinctive point of view:

"He (the author) has been repeatedly cautioned, kindly and unkindly, intelligently and unintelligently, against his alleged tendency to confuse recognised standards of morality by extenuating lives of recklessness, and often criminality, with a single solitary virtue. He might easily show that he has never written a sermon, that he has never moralised or commented upon the actions of his heroes, that he has never voiced a creed or obtrusively demonstrated an ethical opinion. He might easily allege that this merciful effect of his art arose from the reader's weak human sympathies, and hold himself irresponsible. But he would be conscious of a more miserable weakness in thus divorcing himself from his fellow-men who in the domain of art must ever walk hand in hand with him. So he prefers to say that, of all the various forms in which cant presents itself to suffering humanity, he knows of none so outrageous, so illogical, so undemonstrable, so marvellously absurd, as the cant of 'Too Much Mercy.' When it shall be proven to him that communities are degraded and brought to guilt and crime, suffering or destitution, from a predominance of this quality; when he shall see pardoned ticket-of-leave men elbowing men of austere lives out of situation and position, and the repentant Magdalen supplanting the blameless virgin in society—then he will lay aside his pen and extend his hand to the new Draconian discipline in fiction. But until then he will, without claiming to be a religious man or a moralist, but simply as an artist, reverently and humbly conform to the rules laid down by a Great Poet who created the parable of the 'Prodigal Son' and the 'Good Samaritan,' whose works have lasted eighteen hundred years, and will remain when the present writer and his generation are forgotten."

One reads this passage with qualified satisfaction. Based upon a right feeling of indignation, it succeeds in being both didactic and sentimental. When Bret Harte wrote "The Luck of Roaring Camp" and "The Outcasts of Poker Flat" he had a strong instinct to tell the bare truth about human life as he knew it in California. He had also, for better or worse, a decided instinct to invest human nature, in whatsoever dubious guise he might find it, with certain attributes of ideal grace. The resultant of these two impulses was sometimes effective, sometimes merely confusing.

Apart from questions of substance and morals, these first stories possessed another claim upon public interest. The writer had an unmistakable touch of his own. It is during this period that we feel sure of the sincerity of this touch; the earlier stories are patent imitations of Irving and Dickens, and the later, most of them, are as patent imitations of himself. It is not generally known that Bret Harte had been, long before he received Mr. Fields's letter about "The Luck," a contributor to *The Atlantic*. As early as 1863 "The Legend of Monte del Diablo" had appeared in its columns. It was a graceful and spirited sketch, but one can understand easily enough why neither this Spanish-American tale nor its subsequent companions in the same vein excited any especial interest. They are obviously and successfully imitative of Irving, not only in their general atmosphere and treatment, but in their very idioms and cadences. Just as in his earlier character-stories Bret Harte instinctively imitated Dickens, in these sketches he insensibly fell into the mood and manner of the chronicler of the Alhambra, whose spell was still fresh upon the world.

Here, for example, is the opening passage from "The Legend of Monte del Diablo":

"For many years after Father Juni-
pero Serro first rang his bell in the wil-
derness of Upper California, the spirit
which animated that adventurous priest
did not wane. The conversion of the
heathen went on rapidly in the establish-
ment of missions throughout the land.
So sedulously did the good Fathers set
about their work that around their iso-
lated chapels there presently arose adobe
huts, whose mud-plastered and savage
tenants partook regularly of the provi-
sions, and occasionally of the Sacrament,
of their pious hosts. Nay, so great was
their progress, that one zealous Padre is
reported to have administered the Lord's
Supper on Sabbath morning to 'over
three hundred heathen salvages.' It was

not to be wondered that the Enemy of Souls, being greatly incensed thereat, and alarmed at his decreasing popularity, should have grievously tempted and embarrassed these holy Fathers, as we shall presently see.

"Yet they were happy, peaceful days for California. The vagrant keels of prying Commerce had not as yet ruffled the lordly gravity of her bays. No torn and ragged gulch betrayed the suspicion of golden treasure. The wild oats drooped idly in the morning heat or wrestled with the afternoon breezes. Deer and antelope dotted the plain. The water-courses brawled in their familiar channels, nor dreamed of shifting their regular tide. The wonders of the Yosemite and Calaveras were as yet unrecorded. The holy Fathers noted little of the landscape beyond the barbaric prodigality with which the quick soil repaid the sowing. A new conversion, the advent of a saint's day, or the baptism of an Indian baby was at once the chronicle and marvel of their day.

"At this blissful epoch there lived at the Mission of San Pablo Father José Antonio Haro, a worthy brother of the Society of Jesus. He was of tall and cadaverous aspect. A somewhat romantic history had given a poetic interest to his lugubrious visage. While a youth, pursuing his studies at famous Salamanca, he had become enamoured of the charms of Doña Carmen de Torrence-

vara as that lady passed to her matutinal
devotions. Untoward circumstances, has-
tened perhaps by a wealthier suitor,
brought this amour to a disastrous issue,
and Father José entered a monastery,
taking upon himself the vows of celibacy.
It was here that his natural fervour and
poetic enthusiasm conceived expression as
a missionary. A longing to convert the
uncivilised heathen succeeded his frivolous
earthly passion, and a desire to explore
and develop unknown fastnesses continually possessed him. In his flashing eye
and sombre exterior was detected a singular commingling of the discreet Las
Casas and the impetuous Balboa."

The early stories of modern California
life are as clearly studies after Dickens.

Here, for instance, is a bit of dialogue from "M'liss," which was written while Harte was still a compositor on *The Golden Era:*

"Suddenly she threw herself forward, calling on God to strike her dead, and fell quite weak and helpless with her face on the master's desk, crying and sobbing as if her heart would break.

"The master lifted her gently, and waited for the paroxysm to pass. When, with face still averted, she was repeating between her sobs the *mea culpa* of childish penitence—that 'she'd be good, she didn't mean to,' etc.—it came to him to ask her why she had left Sabbath-school.

"Why had she left Sabbath-school? Why? Oh, yes. What did he (McSnag-

ley) want to tell her she was wicked for?
What did he tell her God hated her for?
If God hated her, what did she want to
go to Sabbath-school for? She didn't
want to be beholden to anybody who
hated her.

"Had she told McSnagley this?

"Yes, she had.

"The master laughed. It was a hearty
laugh, and echoed so oddly in the little
school-house, and seemed so inconsistent
and discordant with the sighing of the
pines without, that he shortly corrected
himself with a sigh. The sigh was quite
as sincere in its way, however, and after
a moment of serious silence he asked
about her father.

"Her father. What father? Whose

father? What had he ever done for her?
Why did the girls hate her? Come, now!
What made the folks say, 'Old Bummer
Smith's M'liss,' when she passed? Yes;
oh, yes. She wished he was dead—she
was dead—everybody was dead; and her
sobs broke forth anew."

Harte's mimetic faculty was already
being deliberately exercised, as the "Condensed Novels," published in 1867,
showed. We may, in this connection,
quote the opening paragraphs of his deliberate parody of Dickens, which he
called, "The Haunted Man: A Christmas
Story":

"Don't tell me that it wasn't a knocker.
I had seen it often enough, and I ought
to know. So ought the three o'clock beer,

in dirty high-lows, swinging himself over the railing, or executing a demoniacal jig upon the door-step; so ought the butcher, although butchers as a general thing are scornful of such trifles; so ought the postman, to whom knockers of the most extravagant description were merely human weaknesses, that were to be pitied and used. And so ought for the matter of that, etc., etc., etc.

"But then it was *such* a knocker. A wild, extravagant, and utterly incomprehensible knocker. A knocker so mysterious and suspicious that policeman 437, first coming upon it, felt inclined to take it instantly in custody, but compromised with his professional instincts by sharply and sternly noting it with an eye that ad-

mitted of no nonsense, but confidently
expected to detect its secret yet. An ugly
knocker; a knocker with a hard, human
face, that was a type of the harder human
face within. A human face that held between its teeth a brazen rod. So here-
after, in the mysterious future, should be
held, etc., etc.

"But if the knocker had a fierce human
aspect in the glare of day, you should
have seen it at night, when it peered out
of the gathering shadows and suggested
an ambushed figure; when the light of the
street-lamps fell upon it, and wrought a
play of sinister expression in its hard out-
lines; when it seemed to wink meaningly
at a shrouded figure who, as the night fell
darkly, crept up the steps and passed into

the mysterious house; when the swinging door disclosed a back passage into which the figure seemed to lose itself and become a part of the mysterious gloom; when the night grew boisterous and the fierce wind made furious charges at the knocker, as if to wrench it off and carry it away in triumph. Such a night as this.

"It was a wild and pitiless wind. A wind that had commenced life as a gentle country zephyr, but, wandering through manufacturing towns, had become demoralised, and, reaching the city, had plunged into extravagant dissipation and wild excesses. A roistering wind that indulged in Bacchanalian shouts on the street-corners, that knocked off the hats from the heads of helpless passengers, and then fulfilled its duties by speeding away, like all young prodigals—to sea."

This is a purer example of parody than Bret Harte commonly produced. As a rule his imitations are of the broad burlesque order, when they are not the instruments of satire.

We have taken pains to note how closely a young writer reproduced the style of the two popular authors to whom he was most nearly akin in temperament. But there was nothing strange in this: the odd thing is that he should have somewhat abruptly emerged from this imitative habit with a style of his own. It was never an altogether pure or good style. That was a day of loose and "picturesque" writing, and Bret Harte, with his journalistic training and self-cultivated taste, was not exempt from the vices of the period. But in that best mood of his, his style did possess a primary integrity; it did express the writer as he was. So far as the faculty of expressing his own personality could so constitute him, Bret Harte was an artist: not of the most refined type, for his nature was not of marked refinement; not of the most powerful type, for he was not a great man.

He is said to have taken great pains with the form of his work. "His writing materials," says Mr. Noah Brooks, "the light and heat, and even the adjustment of the furniture of the writing-room, must be as he desired, otherwise he could not get on with his work. Even when his environment was all that he could wish, there were times when the divine afflatus would not come and the day's work must be abandoned."

Mr. C. W. Stoddard, another friend of the California days, gives similar testimony: "One day I found him pacing the floor of his office, knitting his brows and staring at vacancy. I considered why. He was watching and waiting for a word, the right word, the one word to fit into a line of recently written prose. I suggested one: it would not answer; it must be a word of two syllables, or the natural rhythm of the sentence would suffer. Thus he perfected his prose."

All this is doubtless true; yet the fact remains that Bret Harte never compassed a pure style. With all his efforts toward form he never could make himself a writer of distinction. His style lacks firmness and consistency much as his life lacked these qualities; it lacks refinement, precisely as his nature lacked refinement. With all his particularity in the choice of words he could only use them as counters. He had no sense of language as an organism, and his diction is consequently often conventional, inflated, or coarse. The same thing is true with regard to larger questions of treatment. What (to cite a single instance) could be more popularly effective, what could be in worse taste, than the melodramatic dénouement of "The Luck of Roaring Camp," otherwise so masterly a sketch? There is a similar touch of conventionality in the ending of "Tennessee's Partner," and of more than one other of the famous early stories. They have, in fact, a dual and somewhat conflicting character as sketches and as tales. Harte wished to record the truth, but it was his instinct to give the truth a conventionally ideal turn; and perhaps the commentator who called him a "realistic idealist" came about as near classifying him as one can come.

In his treatment of character we are confronted with the same puzzling contrasts between the sincere and the meretricious. What characterisation more fine, strong, and simple than that of

M'liss, Yuba Bill, Tennessee's Partner, and Miggles? What more set and meretricious than that of the Oakhursts, Starbottles, Hamlins, and the procession of furbelowed creatures, all eyes and ankles, who represent Bret Harte's conception of womanhood? It has been often asserted not only that Harte was a great artist, but that he was a great student of character. In both instances his achievement was inevitably compromised by the limitations of his personality. A certain direct, humourous acceptance of the ruder conditions of frontier life seems to have been his most valuable asset: this and a remarkable instinctive faculty for conveying his impressions. He was, however, keen to see what was picturesque and spectacular in the more complex aspects of that life; and this impression, for whatever it might be worth, he was also able to convey. He worked, in short, under that complication of motives which has proved the undoing of so many born story-writers: the instinct to portray and the instinct to amuse. In the end—and, alas, long before the end— the latter instinct was completely victorious.

According to his own account, it was his purpose from the outset to aid in founding "a distinctive Western American literature," and he appears to have thought that he had actually achieved this. His treatment of the character of Jack Hamlin suggests very well his limitation as an interpreter of Western life.

The spirit of the mining camp he certainly did embody in literature. Otherwise, he was interested in the people who live in the Far West, and in the things which happen there, as a connoisseur in the materials of fiction rather than as a passionate student. We do not, of course, ask for statistics, or a complete philosophy, or a long face, from the creative artist. Mr. Owen Wister has offered us none of these things. Yet by his interpretation of ranch life he has contrived, in the very act of pleasing us, to make us think. Bret Harte was content to make us wonder. He was not greatly concerned that his reading of that life should be profoundly significant; it must be picturesque. Mr. Jack Hamlin is a rascal under a film of smooth manners. Part of his attractiveness consists in our knowledge of his rascality, a lure a good many centuries older than Jack Hamlin or Jack Sheppard. Owen Wister's Virginian is a gentleman under a coat of roughness. This also is an immemorial type of hero. So far as they are private persons, it is proper that we should get as much pleasure out of one type as out of the other. But we can, after all, hardly yield to Jack Hamlin and the Virginian the immunities of private life. If the phenomena of the West really interest us, we shall find ourselves considering the claims of each in turn to be taken as representative of the frontier phase of civilisation. Weighed in such a mood, Mr. Jack Hamlin, with all his fascinations, is found wanting; one must be lightly pleased with him, or not at all. The Virginian (who will never become as famous as Mr. Hamlin) is far more edifying; he is much more nearly in the line of descent from those strong frontiersmen of Bret Harte's earliest work.

Even that work was not, it is plain, based upon a conscious philosophy. He had no faculty of subtle analysis; he did have a crude, strong understanding of the crude, strong frontier life. The flavour of that life has best been suggested, so far as generalisation is concerned, by a dweller in the Bret Harte country: "Somehow the rawness of the land favours the sense of personal relation to the supernatural. There is not much interven-

tion of crops, cities, clothes, and manners
between you and the organising forces
to cut off communication. All this begets
in Jimville a state that passes explanation
unless you will accept an explanation that
passes belief. Along with killing and
drunkenness, coveting of women, charity,
simplicity, there is a certain indifference,
blankness, emptiness, if you will, of all
vapourings, no bubbling of the pot—it
wants the German to coin a word for
that—no bread-envy, no brother-fervour.
. . . It is pure Greek in that it repre-
sents the courage to shear off what is not
worth while. Beyond that it endures
without snivelling, renounces without
self-pity, fears no death, rates itself not
too great in the scheme of things; so do

beasts, so did St. Jerome in the desert, so also in the elder day did the gods. Life, its performance, cessation, is no new thing to gape and wonder at." *

It is of life taken in this spirit that Bret Harte first offered a reasonable interpretation. Since then, by Kipling, by Owen Wister, and by other hands, the feat has been often repeated. Bret Harte had no other interpretation to offer. He had no power of making sophistication interesting. Consequently his removal to the East and to Europe did not, as happened with Mr. Henry James, open a new career for him. He did not understand the life of the common people in

* Jimville: A Bret Harte Town. Mary Austin, in *The Atlantic Monthly*, November, 1902.

Germany or England; and he utterly failed in attempting to portray a lady or a gentleman of any race.

Apart from his purely creative work something remains to be said of him as a satirist. His satirical impulse found two modes of expression: in humourous verse and in prose parody. He was capable of good serious verse. As early as 1865 he had published a volume of somewhat pretentious romantic poems, which attracted rather less attention than it deserved. Even earlier than this, however, he had hit upon his real vein in "The Society upon the Stanislaus," in which Truthful James and his artless method of moralising appeared for the first time. But it remained for his later narrative about the Heathen Chinee to make the name of Truthful James famous. The explanation of the greater vogue of the latter poem lies not only in the prestige which now belonged to the author of "The Luck," but in the more strikingly satirical quality of the poem itself. The swarming of the Chinese upon the Pacific Slope had already become a "question." "Chinese cheap labour" had begun to be a war-cry; and Bret Harte, with his instinct for the concrete, had hit upon an illustration of the problem at once astonishingly simple and astonishingly strong. The whole problem of this difficulty between East and West is embodied in the game of euchre

BRET HARTE

between Truthful James, Bill Nye, and
the innocent Ah Sin:

"Which we had a small game,
And Ah Sin took a hand;
It was euchre.   The same
He did not understand;
But he smiled as he sat by the table,
With a smile that was childlike and bland.

"Yet the cards they were stacked
In a way that I grieve,
And my feelings were shocked
At the state of Nye's sleeve:
Which was stuffed full of aces and bowers,
And the same with intent to deceive.

"But the hands that were played
By that heathen Chinee,
And the points that were made

[112]

WORK

Were quite frightful to see,—
Till at last he put down a right bower,
   Which the same Nye had dealt unto me.

"Then I looked up at Nye,
   And he gazed upon me,
And he rose with a sigh,
   And said, 'Can this be?
We are ruined by Chinese cheap labour;'
   And he went for that heathen Chinee.

"In the scene that ensued
   I did not take a hand;
But the floor it was strewed
   Like the leaves on the strand
With the cards that Ah Sin had been hiding
   In the game he did not understand.

"In his sleeves, which were long,
   He had twenty-four packs,—
Which was coming it strong,

BRET HARTE

Yet I state but the facts;
And we found on his nails, which were taper,
What's frequent in tapers—that's wax.

"Which is why I remark,
And for tricks that are vain,
And my language is plain,
That for ways that are dark,
The heathen Chinee is peculiar,—
Which the same I am free to maintain."

What is there omitted in this as a study of international relations? The duplicity of Bill Nye, his righteous Occidental indignation at the superior duplicity of his adversary, and the complacent moralising of Truthful James himself constitute this poem a consummate piece of satire.

The verses were the more effective from

[114]

the oddity of their metrical structure. They were built, by his own confession, in whimsical imitation of the stately threnody in Swinburne's "Atalanta in Calydon." Harte is said to have illustrated the similarity by alternating the lines in this way:

"Atalanta, the fairest of women, whose name is a
blessing to speak—
Yet he played it that day upon William and me in
a way I despise—
The narrowing Symplegades whitened the straits
of Propontis with spray—
And we found on his nails which were taper, what's
frequent in tapers—that's wax."

It is to be noted that the elements of satire and parody are both present in this most famous of Bret Harte's metrical experiments; and it was in the employment of these elements that he longest maintained his strength. He never achieved another "Heathen Chinee," but his first prose volume was a series of "Condensed Novels," and so was his last.

Somebody said, during the period of Bret Harte's undoing at the hands of Eastern admirers, that his genius was "a lead and not a pocket." This was precisely untrue, as he presently proved to the world's satisfaction. His pocket made him rich in a day; his lead barely yielded pay-ore. When he died one journal said that the world had lost one of its most beloved authors. Another said that neither the world nor literature had lost anything by his death. Both remarks are true. "The Luck of Roaring Camp" gave him standing with Goldsmith and Sterne and Irving and Dickens and all the glorious company of the writers of sentiment. But his art did not grow; it consequently did not hold its own. He was not a consummate artist, he was not a commanding personality. One thing he did admirably, and the world is in no danger of forgetting him.

THE END

[117]